"Law and Order: Exploring the Foundations of Society" Tracing the Evolution of Legal Systems and Their Impact on Civilization

James Harris

All right reserved. No part of this publication may be reproduced, distributed, or transmitted in any form or by any means, including photocopying, recording, or other electronic or mechanical methods, without the prior written permission of the publisher, except in the case of brief quotations embodied in critical reviews and certain other non-commercial uses permitted by copyright law.

Copyright © James Harris, 2024

Table of contents
Chapter 1
Chapter 2
Chapter 3
Chapter 4
Chapter 5

Chapter 1

Ancient Origins of Law

In the first chapter of this book, we will begin an exciting adventure to investigate the roots of law. We will trace the genealogy of law through the ancient civilizations of Mesopotamia, Egypt, and Greece. The legal systems that are the foundation of contemporary jurisprudence were established by these early cultures, which created the cornerstone for those systems. By studying their laws, rituals, and philosophies, we can obtain a deeper understanding of the everlasting search for justice and order that has been the driving force behind the development of human civilization.

The Codes of Mesopotamia: Hammurabi and Additional Codes

Mesopotamia, which is sometimes considered to be the birthplace of civilization, hosted some of the first legal laws that are now known to exist. Of them, the Code of Hammurabi, which was created by the Babylonian monarch Hammurabi about the year 1754 BCE, stands out as a law text that is considered to be of fundamental importance.

Hammurabi's Code, which was written on a stele and exhibited in a public place for everyone to see, was an attempt to control every area of Mesopotamian society, from business and property rights to family affairs and the administration of civil and criminal justice. Its premise of lex talionis, which translates to "an eye for an eye," recalls the ancient belief in the use of proportionate punishment as a way of preserving social order.

Nevertheless, Hammurabi's efforts were not the only ones. Additionally, across Mesopotamia, various city-states produced their very own legal codes, each of which was adapted to meet the particular requirements and principles of their culture. The Law Code of Ur-Nammu, dating back to the 21st century BCE, and the Law Code of Lipit-Ishtar are important instances of early legal systems that precede Hammurabi's Code.

These legal codes, albeit less well-preserved than Hammurabi's, give unique insights into the legal norms and practices of ancient Mesopotamia.

Egyptian Legal Traditions: Ma'at and Justice

In ancient Egypt, the notion of Ma'at, typically translated as "truth," "order," or "justice," served as the cornerstone of the judicial system. Ma'at signified the divine order of the cosmos, embodying the ideals of harmony, balance, and cosmic justice. Maintaining Ma'at was not just a religious responsibility but also a social one, since it secured the stability and prosperity of Egyptian society.

The judicial system of ancient Egypt was tightly linked with religious beliefs and rites. The pharaoh, considered to be the heavenly ruler anointed by the gods, was bestowed with ultimate power over law and justice. Under the pharaoh's power, a hierarchy of judges, scribes, and administrators administered the law, resolved disputes, and enforced decisions. The "Book of the Dead," a collection of funerary literature, has chapters that picture the departed facing trial in the afterlife, where their deeds in life are assessed against the principles of Ma'at.

Greek Philosophers and the Birth of Legal Thought

In ancient Greece, the pursuit of justice and the essence of law captivated the thoughts of philosophers and academics. Greek scholars such as Socrates, Plato, and Aristotle struggled with concerns of ethics, morality, and government, providing the framework for Western legal theory.

Socrates, famed for his style of questioning and critical inquiry, questioned traditional views of fairness and attempted to find the fundamental elements of morality. His trial and subsequent death in 399 BCE, as described in Plato's "Apology," underlined the conflict between individual conscience and the power of the state.

Plato, in his writings such as "The Republic" and "Laws," envisioned an ideal society controlled by philosopher-kings who rule by reason and fairness. He investigated the notion of justice as harmony and advocated for the education and moral training of people as important elements for a fair society.

Aristotle, a pupil of Plato, advocated a more pragmatic approach to law and administration in his writings "Nicomachean Ethics" and "Politics." He considered legislation as a method of advancing the common good and creating virtuous citizenship. Aristotle's distinction between distributive and corrective justice set the framework for subsequent legal thinkers and practitioners.

As we complete our investigation of the ancient beginnings of law, we are reminded of the continuing impact of these early civilizations and their contributions to the creation of legal systems. From the codified rules of Mesopotamia to the divine justice of ancient Egypt and the philosophical investigations of ancient Greece, the yearning for justice and order has been a recurring theme throughout human history.

In the chapters that follow, we will go further into the development of law, studying its role in building societies, settling disputes, and maintaining the rights and obligations of people.

Chapter 2

Medieval Legal Systems

As we delve further into the annals of legal history, Chapter 2 uncovers the rich fabric of medieval legal systems. A time distinguished by chaotic political landscapes, religious fervor, and social reconstruction, the Middle Ages saw the creation of legal systems that would profoundly alter the trajectory of European history. From the advent of feudalism to the impact of canon law, this chapter highlights the complex character of law throughout this transformational age.

Feudalism and the Development of Common Law:

The loss of central authority after the fall of the Roman Empire pushed Europe into a period of decentralization and fragmentation. In this vacuum, feudalism arose as a dominating socio-economic system, marked by the exchange of land for loyalty and military service. Within the feudal order, lords exercised power over their vassals, delivering justice via regional manorial courts.

Amidst the fragmented government of medieval Europe, the seeds of common law started to grow in England. Common law, anchored on customary practices and local precedent, increasingly displaced the patchwork of feudal laws. Itinerant judges traveled the countryside, adjudicating conflicts and promulgating verdicts that became binding legal precedents. The formation of royal courts, such as the Court of Common Pleas and the Court of King's Bench, offered a centralized platform for the settlement of legal problems, supporting the development of a unified legal system.

The Magna Carta of 1215 serves as a cornerstone of medieval legal history, marking the supremacy of the rule of law over arbitrary monarchical power.

Enshrining concepts of due process and restricting the powers of the king, the Magna Carta established the framework for constitutional government and the preservation of individual liberty.

Canon Law and the Influence of Religion:

In combination with secular legal systems, medieval Europe was regulated by the imperatives of canon law, the ecclesiastical jurisprudence of the Catholic Church. Canon law, drawn from biblical principles and papal decrees, penetrated all elements of medieval society, exercising influence on topics of morality, marriage, and inheritance.

Canon law tribunals, presided over by ecclesiastical authority, exercised enormous influence in questions of religious doctrine and discipline. The pope, as the highest judge of canon law, exerted authority over bishops, clergy, and faithful equally, enforcing compliance with church doctrines and orthodoxy.

The Influence of Legal Traditions on Society:

The legal systems of medieval Europe significantly altered the fabric of society, defining power relations, social hierarchies, and cultural standards. Feudal law formalized the ties between lords and vassals, while common law offered a method for settling disputes and sustaining community order. Canon law, filled with spiritual power, penetrated all parts of life, influencing moral behavior and religious activity.

As Chapter 2 concludes, we are left with a strong appreciation for the intricacy and variety of medieval legal systems. From the decentralized government of feudalism to the spiritual imperatives of canon law, these legal systems exercised a tremendous impact on the course of European history.

In the chapters that follow, we will continue our examination of legal development, following the features of jurisprudence through the epochs of Renaissance humanism, Enlightenment philosophy, and contemporary constitutionalism.

Chapter 3

Foundations of Modern Legal Systems

This chapter dives into the roots of contemporary legal systems, tracking the growth of jurisprudence from the Enlightenment period to the current day. As civilizations experienced major alterations in the wake of political revolutions, scientific discoveries, and cultural upheavals, legal thinking and practice changed to meet the shifting requirements of a more complex and linked society. This chapter analyzes the formation of civil law and common law traditions, the codification of legal ideas, and the establishment of international legal frameworks that continue to affect the global legal environment.

Civil Law vs. Common Law: A Comparative Analysis

The Enlightenment period saw a developing interest in logical inquiry, individual rights, and the pursuit of societal improvement. In Europe, this intellectual ferment gave birth to two separate legal traditions: civil law and common law. Civil law, founded in Roman jurisprudence and codified laws, stresses the importance of legislation and court precedent in creating legal decisions. Common law, by contrast, depends on court judgments and legal precedents to interpret and implement the law, producing a dynamic and changing legal system.

Central to civil law systems is the notion of legal codes, complete collections of legislation and regulations that control all elements of civil and criminal law. Civil law regimes, such as those found in continental Europe and Latin America, promote legal clarity and predictability, with courts concerned largely with the administration of existing laws rather than the formation of new legal concepts.

In common law regimes, judges have a more active role in establishing legal theory via the interpretation of legislation and the formation of case law. The idea of stare decisis, or precedent, provides consistency and continuity in legal decision-making while allowing for flexibility and adaptability to changing societal norms and values. Common law regimes, like the United Kingdom, the United States, and former British colonies, emphasize judicial reasoning and the growth of legal ideas via judicial review and appellate procedures.

Constitutionalism and the Rule of Law

At the core of contemporary legal systems is the notion of constitutionalism, the belief in the supremacy of written constitutions as the highest law of the state. The Enlightenment ideas of popular sovereignty, individual liberties, and limited government found expression in the constitutional frameworks of the late 18th and early 19th centuries.

Constitutions act as bulwarks against arbitrary governmental authority, establishing the rights and obligations of individuals and the systems of government. Through measures such as separation of powers, checks and balances, and judicial review, constitutionalism strives to defend individual freedoms and promote democratic government.

International Law: From Sovereignty to Global Governance

The 20th century saw the rise of international law as a unique and prominent subject of legal investigation. In an increasingly linked world, the need for rules and standards to control interactions between states and non-state entities became important.

International law comprises a vast variety of legal instruments and structures, including treaties, conventions, and international organizations such as the United Nations and the International Court of Justice. via concepts such as sovereignty, state accountability, and human rights, international law attempts to promote peace, collaboration, and the settlement of disputes via peaceful means.

As Chapter 3 concludes, we are left with a strong appreciation for the roots of contemporary legal systems and their continuing effect on the administration of societies across the globe. From the codification of civil law principles to the growth of common law doctrines and the formation of international legal standards, the struggle for justice and the rule of law continues to motivate legal thinking and practice in the 21st century.

Chapter 4

Legal Institutions and Processes

This chapter dives into the intricacy of legal institutions and procedures, which serve as the cornerstones of government in contemporary countries. These institutions, including the judiciary, the legislative branch, and the executive, play crucial responsibilities in preserving the rule of law, defending individual rights, and guaranteeing the smooth running of democratic regimes. via a detailed investigation of their roles, structures, and relationships, this chapter offers insight into the methods via which laws are formed, interpreted, and enforced.

The Judiciary: Guardians of Justice

The judiciary serves as the cornerstone of every legal system, charged with the sacred responsibility of interpreting and implementing the law. Composed of judges and courts at different levels, the judiciary acts as the unbiased arbitrator of conflicts, ensuring that justice is administered fairly and in conformity with established legal norms.

Judges, appointed or elected depending on the jurisdiction, can interpret laws, mediate disagreements, and adjudicate disputes. Guided by legal precedent, statutory law, and constitutional principles, judges play a critical role in defending individual rights, restraining governmental abuse of power, and maintaining the rule of law.

From trial courts to appellate courts, the judiciary functions within a hierarchical structure, with higher courts holding the jurisdiction to review judgments issued by lower courts. Through this system of judicial review, legal consistency and coherence are preserved, assuring uniformity in the implementation of the law.

Legislative Processes: Crafting Laws for Society

In democratic countries, the legislative arm of government is responsible for the design and adoption of laws that represent the will and values of the people. Comprising elected officials who serve in legislative bodies such as parliaments or congresses, the legislature plays a crucial role in defining the legal framework of society.

The legislative process is defined by discussion, debate, and negotiation, as politicians introduce, alter, and vote on laws addressing a broad variety of social concerns. Bills may originate from individual politicians, government agencies, or public advocacy organizations, undergoing review and refinement via committee hearings and floor discussions before being adopted into law.

Executive Powers and Checks and Balances

The executive arm of government, led by the chief executive, is entrusted with enacting and enforcing the laws approved by the legislative. In parliamentary systems, the executive may consist of a prime minister and cabinet ministers, who are responsible to the legislature and serve at its discretion. In presidential systems, the executive is led by a directly elected president, who acts as both head of state and head of government.

Despite their great powers, executive authorities are subject to checks and balances to avoid abuse of power and maintain accountability. Constitutional processes, such as separation of powers, judicial review, and parliamentary scrutiny, act as protections against executive excess and maintain the norms of democratic government.

As Chapter 4 concludes, we are reminded of the crucial role played by legal institutions and procedures in sustaining the rule of law and developing democratic government.

From the judiciary's dedication to impartiality and fairness to the legislature's role in developing laws that represent the goals of society, each department of government contributes to the operation of a healthy legal system.

Chapter 5

The Future of Law

This chapter reveals a captivating story about the future of law, delving into the dynamic interaction of technology innovation, social transformation, and legal progress. As we stand on the verge of a new age, defined by unparalleled breakthroughs and global interconnection, this chapter strives to negotiate the complications and opportunities that lie ahead for legal systems worldwide.

From the transformational potential of artificial intelligence to the urgency of tackling serious social and environmental concerns, the future of law promises to be both thrilling and riddled with uncertainty.

The Role of Artificial Intelligence and Automation

Artificial intelligence (AI) is poised to alter the legal profession, bringing new prospects for efficiency, accuracy, and creativity. AI-powered solutions, such as natural language processing, predictive analytics, and automated document review, are already altering legal research, contract drafting, and case management operations.

By embracing the potential of AI, attorneys, and legal professionals may expedite repetitive processes, freeing up time for higher-order thinking, strategic analysis, and client-centered services. From predictive modeling to aid with case strategy to chatbots offering legal information to the public, AI has the potential to democratize access to justice and better the delivery of legal services.

However, the growth of AI also creates complicated ethical and legal difficulties, including worries about algorithmic bias, data privacy, and the displacement of human jobs. As legal systems cope with these concerns, politicians, attorneys, and technologists must work jointly to define ethical norms, transparency standards, and regulatory frameworks that assure the appropriate and fair deployment of AI in the legal arena.

Globalization and the Changing Nature of Legal Practice

In an age of unparalleled globalization, legal practice is rapidly crossing national borders, requiring lawyers to traverse multiple legal systems, cultural norms, and regulatory frameworks. Globalization has aided the internationalization of legal services, allowing law firms to develop worldwide networks, extend their customer base, and cooperate across boundaries.

However, globalization also offers obstacles, including harmonizing various legal regimes, settling cross-border conflicts, and addressing concerns of jurisdictional uncertainty. As legal practice becomes increasingly linked and interdisciplinary, attorneys must build cross-cultural competency, flexibility, and agility to flourish in a quickly changing global context.

The Imperative of Social Justice and Environmental Sustainability

As the globe grapples with urgent social and environmental concerns, legal institutions are increasingly relied upon to play a crucial role in promoting social justice and environmental sustainability. From tackling structural inequality and discrimination to addressing climate change and environmental degradation, attorneys have a key role to play in pushing for systemic changes and policy initiatives that enhance the common good.

By using the power of law and activism, attorneys may defend human rights, civil freedoms, and environmental safeguards, holding governments and businesses responsible for their actions. From fighting historic cases to crafting legislation and organizing grassroots movements, legal professionals have the power to affect dramatic change and design a more fair and sustainable future for everyone.

As Chapter 5 concludes, we are left with a strong feeling of both excitement and fear for the future of law. In an age of extraordinary technological innovation, globalization, and social change, legal systems must adapt and grow to meet the increasing requirements and problems of society.

By embracing innovation, supporting ethical values, and advocating social justice, attorneys and legal professionals may help pave the path for a better and more equitable future for generations to come.

www.ingramcontent.com/pod-product-compliance
Lightning Source LLC
Chambersburg PA
CBHW050255230526
45470CB00005B/2274